A Tribute to
THE YOUNG AT HEART

GERTRUDE CHANDLER WARNER

By Joan Wallner

Published by Abdo & Daughters, 4940 Viking Drive, Suite 622, Edina, Minnesota 55435.

Library bound edition distributed by Rockbottom Books, Pentagon Tower, P.O. Box 36036, Minneapolis, Minnesota 55435.

Printed in the United States.

Cover Photo credit: Margaret Coleman Abdo
Interior Photo credits: Archive Photos, page 15
Bettmann Archives, page 13
Wide World Photos, page 16

Edited by Rosemary Wallner

Wallner, Joan.
Gertrude Chandler Warner / Joan Wallner. p. cm. — (The Young at Heart).
Summary: Discusses the life and career of the writer famous for having created the Boxcar Children.
ISBN 1-56239-520-3
1. Warner, Gertrude Chandler, 1890- —Juvenile literature. 2. Women authors, American—20th century—Biography—Juvenile literature. 3. Children's stories—Authorship—Juvenile literature. [1. Warner, Gertrude Chandler, 1890- . 2. Authors, American. 3. Women—Biography.] I. Title. II. Series: Tribute to the young at heart.
PS3545.A58235G4   1995
813'.52—dc20
[B]   95-23928
                                                                    CIP

                                                                    AC

TABLE OF CONTENTS

WRITING A CHILDHOOD DREAM

Gertrude Chandler Warner loved to teach. But in 1923 she became ill and couldn't work. While she recovered, she decided to write stories for her young students. But she couldn't think of anything to write about.

Warner had always dreamed of living in a freight car. She began to write about four children who lived in an old boxcar. The four characters—Henry, Jessie, Violet, and Benny Alden—became the Boxcar Children. After Warner's book was revised in 1942, people—especially children—wanted more adventures of the Alden children. Warner retired from teaching and wrote 18 more books for the Boxcar Children series. Since those first books, other authors have written about the independent Alden children. The story Warner began that day in 1923 continues today.

GROWING UP NEAR A TRAIN DEPOT

Gertrude Chandler Warner was born on April 16, 1890, in Putnam, a small town in the northeast corner of Connecticut. She lived there her entire life. Little information is known about Warner's parents or her brothers and sisters. Most of what we know about her childhood comes directly from books she wrote as an adult.

When she was young, Warner loved to play with her dollhouse filled with handmade furniture and toy musical instruments. Her favorite instruments were the cello and pipe organ.

Gertrude Chandler Warner, age 10.

She also loved reading books, especially *Alice in Wonderland*. While reading, Warner often dreamt of writing a book. Warner and her sister, Frances, began to write when they were just able to hold a pencil. Letting their imaginations take over, the two sisters wrote their ideas on paper scraps.

Warner's parents, Edgar and Jane Warner, didn't like paper scraps littering their house. So they bought Warner and her sister 10-cent books filled with blank pages.

Writing was easy for Warner because she wrote about things she saw and did. Her favorite subjects were trains.

The Warner home was across the train tracks from the Putnam train depot. Every day, people bought their tickets and boarded the trains.

The Warner's lived so close to the train tracks that they could wave good-bye to friends without leaving their yard. Warner spent hours watching the engines, passenger cars, and freight trains clatter by her house.

When she was older, Warner wrote about the time her brother, Geoffrey, and his wife were boarding the train for their honeymoon. The Warner family said good-bye to them at the depot and walked home to wave from their front yard. But when a freight train came by, it blocked their view of the depot and of Geoffrey.

The Warners rushed to an upstairs window. But a pear tree blocked their view. The family crawled out through the window onto the house's rooftop and began to wave.

Geoffrey, as well as people walking by their house, saw them waving. The family on the roof looked peculiar because people on the street didn't know they were actually waving good-bye to someone.

A FIRE AND HAY FEVER

As a young child, Warner's nose was often stuffed up and she sneezed much of the time. She suffered from hay fever. No medicine could cure it.

One day, the Warner's house caught fire. Everyone in the house ran around excitedly. Once everyone was outside safely, Warner realized her sneezing had stopped. But when all the excitement was over, her sneezing and runny nose started once again.

Warner realized that exciting events stopped her hay fever. But, she wrote, it wasn't possible to burn the house down every time she wanted relief.

Her family created different kinds of excitement to relieve her hay fever symptoms. Through their attempts, Warner found that laughing also helped.

A friend of Geoffrey's often visited the Warner home. He could stop Warner from sneezing by standing on his head. But this remedy was only temporary.

Warner finally decided that she should travel to the mountains or the sea for relief. First, she went to the sea, which was close to her home. She discovered that the sea wind also carried pollen, which had caused her to sneeze at home. Unable to breathe through her nose, she visited the mountains. She didn't have much luck there, either. Hay fever would affect her health the rest of her life.

CHOOSING A CAREER

When Warner was 18 years old, she became restless. She wanted to write books and magazine articles about her childhood and life experiences.

Her mother had a serious talk with Warner and her sister. "It was a nice idea to write," Mrs. Warner told them, "but don't expect to earn any money from it."

"She would be surprised if she knew how wrong she was," Warner said, remembering her mother's words.

At the time, Warner didn't give up her writing dream. She simply set writing aside for a while. She knew she needed more education than just completing grade school and high school.

Warner decided to attend college and looked at many schools near her home. Warner took summer classes at nearby Yale University in New Haven, Connecticut, so she could live at home.

While attending classes, Warner became interested in teaching. She knew she could make a living teaching children.

Southeastern view of Putnam, Connecticut, late 1800s, the
town in which Warner grew up.

PUBLISHING BOOKS AND MAGAZINE ARTICLES

In 1915, Warner found a way to write and teach young children. She decided to write children's books. The following year, at age 25, Warner's first book, *The House of Delight*, was published. The book contained verses illustrated with watercolors.

While writing her second book, Warner faced many decisions, including whether or not to quit Yale University. In 1918, she took a teaching position at Putnam Grade School.

People in Putnam knew Warner had talent. Members of the American Red Cross asked her if she would volunteer her writing skills for their group. She agreed and became the group's publicity chairwoman in 1917. She wrote press

Yale University, where Warner attended classes in 1917.

An American Red Cross military hospital, 1918. Warner
volunteered her time to the Red Cross.

releases to tell local newspapers about Red Cross events. She enjoyed her volunteer work so much that she remained a member her entire life.

Warner knew she couldn't go to school, teach, and volunteer at the same time. She decided not to enroll in classes that summer. Instead, she taught during the day and wrote books at night.

At the time, Warner wrote with a pencil. "I always said I could write better if I had a decent pencil, and this was true," she said. Her house, however, never seemed to have new pencils. She had pencils that had been sharpened with a knife and very, very small ones, but never any new ones.

That summer, Warner published her first magazine article titled, "The Return of A, B, C." It was printed in *The Outlook*.

Each time Warner saw one of her articles or books in print, she knew she wanted to write for the rest of her life. In 1918, her second children's book, *Star Stories*, was published. It was about planets and stars. Warner got the idea for the book when she taught her class about the universe.

Meanwhile, Warner's sister, Frances, was also writing. Her work appeared in *Atlantic Monthly, Education*, and *House Beautiful*. She, too, had published a few books.

The two sisters made plans to write a book for adults. In 1921, *Life's Minor Collisions* was published. The book contained articles and stories that the sisters had previously published in magazines. Warner finally had a successful writing career.

A religious organization in her state asked her to write a series of books for Sunday school classes. Warner wrote eight children's books for churches to use.

THE BOXCAR CHILDREN AND BRONCHITIS

In 1923, Warner could not teach because she had an attack of bronchitis. Her lungs were inflamed and she couldn't breathe normally.

Instead of letting her bad health get her down, Warner made the best of her recovery time. She made the days at home enjoyable by writing, dreaming, and remembering happy times.

She remembered watching the trains go by her house. Many times a caboose would stop in front of her. Peering inside the caboose's window, Warner could see inside the small car. It contained a tiny stove with a stovepipe, a little table, cracked cups with no saucers, and a tin coffee pot boiling water on the stove.

"This sight always made me dream about how fun it would be to live and keep house in a freight car or caboose," Warner said. "Even after I grew up and began to teach school, this seemed like a fine dream."

As Warner grew older, she noticed that cabooses changed their appearance. Wondering why they were different, Warner wrote to Andrew P. Donovan. Donovan was a friend and a retired engineer.

Donovan told her the windows on the caboose weren't different. He then asked her if she wanted to see the inside of a caboose.

"I couldn't think of anything I'd rather do!" Warner replied. When the day came to see the caboose, she was excited.

The caboose was just as she remembered it as a young girl. It even had a little stove and cups with no saucers. "It still seemed like a good idea to live in a caboose," Warner said after her visit.

Warner thought children would enjoy reading a book about living in a train car. With a pencil in her hand, she began to write. She made the book exciting and fun. Her main characters were four orphaned children. While walking through a forest one day, they found an abandoned railroad car. The Alden children made this their new home.

Warner's characters were independent, resourceful, and could live on their own with little adult supervision.

The Boxcar Children was published in 1924 by Rand McNally. At first, few children read the book. Eighteen years later, in 1942, Scott, Foresman & Company revised the book. That's when children across the country began to take interest in the story.

WRITING MORE CHILDHOOD DREAMS

Warner was very pleased with *The Boxcar Children*. She had written about a dream and had made her dream come alive in a book. Never before had she been able to do that. Now she wanted to write more about her dreams.

Between 1927 and 1967, Warner wrote six more children's books: *The World in a Barn, Windows into Alaska, The World on a Farm, Children of the Harvest, 1001 Nights,* and *Peter Piper: A Missionary Parakeet.*

Warner loved to garden and included her gardening experience and knowledge in her books. "At times," she said, "I had beautiful gardens, spaded and planted by me."

Warner mostly wrote articles and books for children. But in 1932, Warner and her sister began talking about publishing another book for adults. The book, *Pleasures and Palaces*, was published in 1933. To the sister's astonishment, a reporter from *The New York Times* reviewed the book. Warner had never imagined that her work would be written about in such a well-known and respected newspaper.

Warner was pleased that people were reading her books. After the review, she wrote two more adult books: *Henry Barnard: An Introduction* in 1937, and *History of Connecticut* in 1938.

With her new success, Warner stopped writing with old pencils, which were difficult to find in her house anyway. Before starting each book, she bought a dozen black Sharpie pens and a hundred-page notebook.

Warner also decorated a special workroom with violet wallpaper. She moved her typewriter, paper cutter, and easy chair into the room. With her workroom in order, Warner continued writing.

CHILDREN DEMAND MORE ADVENTURES

When Scott, Foresman & Company revised the *Boxcar Children* book in 1942, young readers across the country demanded more adventures of the Alden children. The publishing company and Warner received many letters.

Warner talked about the success of her books in a newsletter published by Scott Foresman in 1967. "Perhaps you know that the original Boxcar Children raised a storm of protest from teachers who thought children shouldn't be having such a good time without parental control," Warner said. "But that is exactly why children like it."

The interest in her book thrilled Warner beyond her wildest dreams. She never imagined children would enjoy reading her book so much that they wanted more adventures. Scott Foresman published *Surprise Island*, the second book in the series, in 1949. The books were sent to public libraries and schools.

In 1950, Warner retired from teaching after 32 years. She wanted to please children across the country by writing what they enjoyed reading. Warner and her publisher began a juvenile mystery series.

The Alden children were the main characters in each book. Warner wrote 17 books about their adventures. The mysteries included *The Yellow House Mystery* published in 1953; *Mystery Ranch*, 1958; *Mike's Mystery*, 1960; *Blue Bay Mystery*, 1961; *Woodshed Mystery*, 1962; *The Lighthouse Mystery*, 1963; *The Mountain Top Mystery*, 1964; *The Schoolhouse Mystery*, 1965; *The Caboose Mystery*, 1966; *Houseboat Mystery*,

1967; *Snowbound Mystery*, 1968; *Treehouse Mystery*, 1969; *Bicycle Mystery*, 1970; *Mystery in the Sand*, 1971; *Mystery Behind the Wall*, 1973; *Bus Station Mystery*, 1974; *Benny Uncovers a Mystery*, 1976.

The famous *Boxcar Children Mystery* book cover.

"She was a feisty lady who believed very firmly in what she was doing," said Editor Caroline Rubin in 1992. "She created a family of varying ages so the stories would have wide appeal."

Aside from writing the mystery series, Warner continued volunteering in her hometown. Along with working with her Congregationalist church and the American Red Cross, Warner became the service chairwoman for the Connecticut Cancer Society.

People in Putnam enjoyed working with her. To show their appreciation for her volunteer work, the Emblem Club named Warner "Woman of the Year" in 1965. In 1967, the American National Red Cross gave Warner a 50-year pin and citation for her dedicated work.

WARNER'S LEGACY

When Warner died on August 30, 1979, at age 89, her work stopped. But only for a short time. Demand for more adventures created sales of new stories written by different authors.

Sales of the original *Boxcar Children* hardcover book rose from 12,600 in 1980 to 35,000 in 1988. Then in 1989, Albert Whitman & Company made changes in how Warner's books were printed and sold. Each book before this time was hardcover. The publisher didn't want to print softcover books for fear that it would take away from hardcover book sales.

But the company wanted to meet people's demands for softcover books. So they decided to print the books in hardcover and softcover. In the first year alone, sales for both types of books rose to 170,000.

At the same time, Albert Whitman & Company agreed to let the Scholastic Book Club sell the Boxcar Children series. The book club ignited new interest in the series, increasing sales each year by 50,000.

As children across the country became more and more interested in the series, children, parents, and teachers told Whitman they wanted more mysteries and adventures. The company hired authors to continue Warner's legacy of the Boxcar Children series.

In 1992, the publisher moved its offices. The increased sales volume meant that Whitman needed a larger warehouse.

To meet children's needs and increase interest in the books, cassette tapes were made containing unabridged (the whole book) recordings of some of the original stories.

When Warner sat down to write in 1923, she wanted to create something she would enjoy reading. She never expected her childhood dream would become so popular and continue after her death.

Gertrude Chandler Warner.